JUST A MINUTE

JUST A MINUTE

BIBLICAL REFLECTIONS
FOR BUSY MUMS

Christine Orme

SCRIPTURE UNION

Scripture Union, 207–209 Queensway,
Bletchley, MK2 2EB, England
Email: info@scriptureunion.org.uk
Website: www.scriptureunion.org.uk

Scripture Union Australia
Locked Bag 2, Central Coast Business Centre, NSW 2252
Website: www.su.org.au

Scripture Union USA
P.O. Box 987, Valley Forge, PA 19482
www.scriptureunion.org

British Library Cataloguing-in-Publication Data
A catalogue record for this book is available from the British
Library
Illustrations by Sue Batchelor
Cover design by Five Design.
Printed and bound in Great Britain by Creative Print and Design
(Wales), Ebbw Vale.

👋 Scripture Union is an international Christian charity working with
churches in more than 130 countries, providing resources to bring the good
news about Jesus Christ to children, young people and families and to
encourage them to develop spiritually through the Bible and prayer.

As well as our network of volunteers, staff and associates who run holidays,
church-based events and school Christian groups, we produce a wide range
of publications and support those who use our resources through training
programmes.

For my daughters: Elisabeth, Helen, Ingrid, and Stephanie

ACKNOWLEDGEMENTS

First of all, I should like to thank Andrew Clark of Scripture Union for his encouragement, tact and wisdom throughout this project, and Stuart and Sue Anderson who put me in touch with him. My husband, Eddie, has been as supportive of me in this as he has always been in everything else I've attempted and I want him to know how much I appreciate that. My friends Dorothy Cox, Chris Ledger and Ali Marshall have all read and commented on some of the pieces or allowed me to bounce ideas off them – thank you. Finally, I want to say a big thank-you to Sue Batchelor, a member of my church, who responded without batting an eyelid to my phonecall 'out of the blue', asking if she woud consider doing the illustrations. Sue read and re-read the pieces and went to enormous lengths to find appropriate images for the pieces, whilst working to a very tight time-scale, and I am so grateful for all the trouble she took to get it right.

CONTENTS

Contents

■ PREFACE

It's 8.15 am. You should be *en route* to school. The baby's crying, the phone's ringing and there's someone at the door. You can hear your five-year-old declaiming loudly from upstairs that her reading-book *isn't* under her bed, while, in the kitchen, your two-year-old is spooning the contents of the cat's dish into his wellies with all the focused determination of a Formula One driver. You're desperate for the loo and you haven't done your hair, never mind your face! Distractedly, you notice that someone has opened the door of the hamster cage yet again... *Quiet time?* You must be joking!

I am! The above scenario, with its endless variations – many of which, if printed, would be dismissed as poetic licence (roller-skates in the fridge? potatoes in the washing-machine?) – was part of my life for almost fifteen years: the years I spent at home with one, two or three under-fives, until the fourth and last of my children went to school and, to my amazement, I discovered I had some energy once more.

Brought up on the idea that any day which didn't begin with Bible reading, SU notes and prayer (preferably lengthy and detailed) was doomed to failure, I struggled over those fifteen years, not only with the demands of a young family, but also with guilt arising from the fact that despite my best intentions, I rarely had a proper 'quiet time'. From the moment the first child woke up in the morning to the time the last one went to sleep, there was hardly a moment to myself. I seemed never to finish a sentence, let alone a conversation, and by the end of the day, I was too tired to read my Bible.

I survived, as countless others have done, supported by the Holy Spirit himself, by the love and prayers of husband and friends, and by reflecting during the day on passages of scripture or single verses that I could remember. Praying was done 'on the hoof', often when yet another mini-crisis was looming! Yet I longed to pray more for my children, and for the grace and wisdom to handle them better. Out of that longing, and out of my experience of that frantically busy, energy-sapping calling which is sometimes dismissively described as being 'just a mum', grew the idea for this book: a series of short reflections based on women, mostly mothers, in the Bible; something which mums could read quickly in the morning, to give them something to focus on and pray around during the day.

The Bible speaks to us still about problems we regard as modern. Surrogate parenthood? Infertility? Sibling rivalry? Rebellious teenagers? You read it all there first! 'When your words came, I ate them;' said the prophet (Jeremiah 15:16). My prayer (yes, I have more time for that now!) is that this small book will give you something to 'chew on' during your busy day and a pointer for prayer on a topic related to family life. I really believe that, despite the hard work and frustrations, the pain and the weariness, being a mum is one of the greatest privileges God grants us. May God bless you as you read these reflections.

1 QUESTIONING EVE

'Eve... the mother of all the living.' Genesis 3:20

What was it like
    at the dawning of earth's day?
How did it feel,
    the pair of you in paradise?

Why, Eve, did you,
  of all people, think the grass
would be greener
  if you heeded the serpent?

And why are some
  of us, Eve's daughters, still,
inclined to meddle
  in things that don't concern us?

Lord, deliver me from idle curiosity and from being a busybody. Amen.

GENESIS 2–3

2 GOD SEES: HAGAR

'You are the God who sees me... ' Genesis 16:13

'God-botherers' is a term sometimes used to dismiss those who pray about so-called 'insignificant' matters. However, Jesus himself pointed out that God is concerned even about sparrows (Matthew 10:29–31), and the Bible is full of incidents in which God acts on behalf of the insignificant. Here is one of them.

Sarai, Abram's wife, was barren, so she arranged a surrogate pregnancy, giving her Egyptian slave-girl, Hagar, to Abram. We can perhaps imagine a little how Hagar felt – the words 'used and abused' spring to mind – but she was a slave and this was her lot. It is understandable that, on finding herself pregnant by Abram, she began to despise Sarai. Just for once in her wretched life she was one up on her mistress.

Sarai didn't like this turn of events, blaming Abram even though the idea was originally hers! She started to harass Hagar, who eventually could take no more and ran away, heading for her native Egypt. This is possibly what Sarai intended all along – if Hagar ran away of her own accord, then Sarai could not be accused of turning out a pregnant slave.

This sad, sordid story may ring some bells for you. Have you ever manipulated a situation for your own benefit?

Then God intervened. By a desert spring, Hagar encountered one of his agents. Indeed, the angel 'found Hagar' and knew who she was. He addressed her directly: 'Hagar, servant of Sarai, where have you come from, and where are you going?'

The angel told Hagar to go back and submit to Sarai. This instruction – hard on both counts – was perhaps made easier by the fact that he also told her about her unborn child, naming him Ishmael (meaning 'God hears') and promising that he would be the founder of a great nation.

Hagar, recognising God's intervention, obeyed. Naming the place 'Well of the Living One who sees me' acknowledges her dawning understanding of Abram's God, who met with her when she was at the end of her tether. God 'bothered' with Hagar – an insignificant, abused Egyptian slave-girl.

Sometimes when we are stuck at home with small children, we may also feel insignificant, enslaved even. Hagar's experience encourages us to know that what she discovered can be true for us, too. The 'God who sees' watches over us in love. No detail of our lives escapes his loving concern. Nothing is so small that it cannot be brought to his attention. This is wonderful reassurance both for us and for our children, as I discovered when my own were little. We prayed about all sorts of 'insignificant' matters, including lost pets, and saw God answer.

Find time today to tell God what's bothering you or your children, however insignificant you may feel it is – and expect him to intervene.

Lord, sometimes I feel insignificant and imprisoned at home. Sometimes, like Hagar, I want to run away. Help me to know that I and my children are valuable and significant to you. Help us to bring to you everything that troubles us, however small. Amen.

Pray for mothers who feel trapped by their circumstances, for women who are abused and lacking self-esteem, and for women in the Third World enslaved by poverty and ill-health.

GENESIS 16:1–16

3 TWO KINDS OF LAUGHTER: SARAH

'Sarah laughed to herself... ' Genesis 18:12

Some of Sarah's story overlaps with Hagar's. Even though she had given Hagar to Abraham to ensure that he had an heir, Sarah, still childless, was becoming increasingly bitter. Perhaps Abraham had told her of God's promise that he would be the father of many nations (Genesis 15:1–6) and this rubbed salt into the wound.

One day Abraham was visited by three strangers. He offered them hospitality and Sarah prepared a meal for them, then hid at the entrance to the tent and listened in on their conversation. It turned out that one of the men was the Lord, who repeated his promise to Abraham that Sarah would bear him a son. Sarah could not see how this was possible and laughed to herself: 'After I am worn out and my master is old, will I now have this pleasure?' But God heard her laugh and challenged her – 'Is anything too hard for the Lord?'

Abraham had also laughed when he was first given this promise (Genesis 17:17), but he was not rebuked. Why? I think because Sarah's laughter was disbelieving, the kind of laugh we may indulge in when we feel cynical about something, especially something we may once have believed God would do for us. Instead of holding on in faith, we become disillusioned and bitter, and we laugh because otherwise we would have to admit our disappointment and cry. Such cynicism and bitterness can colour our whole outlook and spill over into family life.

But God is gracious and keeps his promises – and he has the last laugh. Sarah did indeed have a son, Isaac (which means 'he laughs'): 'God has brought me laughter, and everyone who hears about this will laugh with me.'

Have you become disillusioned about something – a prayer God doesn't seem to answer, a promise he hasn't yet fulfilled? Do you ever laugh bitterly about it? Ask God to turn your bitter laughter into the kind of laughter Sarah enjoyed with her small son. Bitter laughter is unhealthy and unhelpful; cheerfulness is good medicine (Proverbs 17:22), as recent medical evidence shows. Laughter is one of God's gifts: let's use it.

Lord, I am finding it hard to feel joy, particularly about .... Please help me to believe your promises and to trust you to bring me to the point where I can say, like Sarah, 'God has brought me laughter.' Amen.

Pray for those who feel disillusioned or let down by God.

GENESIS 18:1–15; 21:1–7

4 GOD HEARS: HAGAR

'God heard the boy crying... ' Genesis 21:17

Children learn attitudes from their parents – in the early years, most often from their mothers. Here it appears that Hagar's dislike of Sarah (Genesis 16:4) was picked up by her son, Ishmael. When Abraham gave a feast to celebrate Isaac's weaning, Ishmael (now a teenager) was caught teasing his young half-brother. Sarah, enraged and protective of Isaac, demanded that Abraham banish both Ishmael and Hagar. Reluctantly, but reassured by God's promise for Ishmael, Abraham sent mother and son away the next day.

I wonder if Hagar thought back to her previous experience of being driven into the desert. Did she remember how God had intervened then? It is sometimes hard to remember God's goodness as we struggle with the latest problem or crisis, isn't it?

Their meagre supplies ran out, and Hagar settled her son in the only shade she could find, then moved away – she could not bear to watch him die. She wept, as any of us would in that situation. But note how God responded here not to the mother, but to the boy's cries of distress.

Again, the angel addressed Hagar directly. He dealt first with her emotions ('Do not be afraid'), then confirmed his promises for Ishmael's future ('I will make him into a great nation'), and finally answered their immediate physical needs ('Then God opened her eyes and she saw a well of water').

There are truths here for us. We can remind ourselves to remember yesterday's answers from God as we face today's crisis. We can also remind ourselves that God loves our children more than we do and is silently planning in love for them. Finally, we can acknowledge that God is able to meet all our emotional, spiritual and physical needs, both long- and short-term; however, he delegates to us the responsibility of meeting many of our children's needs.

What is troubling you today? Perhaps you feel that there is no hope. But God is the God of hope, who can fill us with all joy and peace in believing. Are you facing an impossible situation with a teenager? God is the God of the impossible;

he is more concerned for your teenager than you are. He heard Ishmael's cry of distress; he will hear your teenager's, too.

Father, I come to you today, feeling that I can't even express my fears and despair. Hear my anguish, which goes too deep for words, and show me the way through. Amen.

Pray for any teenagers or parents you know who have problems.

GENESIS 21:8–21

5 FAVOURITISM DOES NO FAVOURS: REBEKAH

'Isaac ... loved Esau, but Rebekah loved Jacob.' Genesis 25:28

From time to time, at moments of stress, each of our four children has said to me accusingly, 'Well, so-and-so is your favourite!' The child mentioned as my favourite has been different each time! Some of us may indeed find one child easier to like than others, perhaps because that child is like us in character. Conversely, we may find a child easier because he or she is *not* like us! However, liking is not the same as loving, which involves wanting the best for each child whether we get on well with them or not. Favouritism in families is a killer, provoking jealousy, sibling rivalry and loss of self-esteem in unfavoured children.

Rebekah began so well! The story of the servant finding a wife for his master's son through God's guidance is the stuff of romance. At first Rebekah – young, beautiful and adventurous enough to ride off into the sunrise (on a camel) to marriage with an unknown bridegroom – was a good wife: Isaac 'loved her; and ... was comforted after his mother's death'.

Twenty years later, Rebekah was still without children. A concerned Isaac prayed, and at last she became pregnant – with twins. Most mothers will recognise the description of their antenatal activity: 'The babies jostled each other within her, and she said, "Why is this happening to me?" So she went to enquire of the Lord.' And God told her that the babies she was carrying would be the founders of two nations, and that the older would serve the younger.

The twins could not have been more different. The older, Esau, loved the outdoor life, and was masculine, hairy and muscular – his father's favourite. Maybe in response to this, Rebekah focused her affection on quiet, stay-at-home Jacob. However, not content to let God's purposes be worked out, Rebekah conspired with her favourite to deceive elderly, blind Isaac and to trick Esau out of his rightful inheritance as the first-born. The outcome was tragic: Esau became determined to kill Jacob in revenge, which led, ironically, to Rebekah losing Jacob and to his long, enforced exile.

Rebekah made two big mistakes. First, she had a favourite. Second, she failed to distinguish between what she could do and what only God could do. Fortunately, God is

greater than our mistakes and our disobedience, and it all came right in the end. But who knows what might have happened if Isaac and Rebekah had not had favourites, and if Rebekah had left things to God?

Like Rebekah, let's take our concerns about our children to the Lord. But let's avoid showing favouritism or manipulating events or our children in our attempts, however well-intentioned, to do God's work for him!

Father, you know that I find .... much easier to like than .... Give me grace to love them equally and to be scrupulously fair in my dealings with them. Help me to trust you to work out their future for them, and deliver me from meddling and manipulation. Amen.

Pray for parents finding it difficult not to have favourites, or trying to handle sibling rivalry.

GENESIS 24; 25:21–34; 27:1–41

6 FAITH MEETS COMMON SENSE: JOCHEBED

'By faith Moses' parents hid him ... and they were not afraid of the king's edict.' Hebrews 11:23

When our children are small, we often find ourselves having to make important decisions about issues that affect them. Because we know that the early years are vital to our children's healthy development, and because we desperately want to 'get it right' all the time, we sometimes agonise over these decisions. Take heart from Jochebed! She is mentioned only twice by name in the Bible, yet she had to make a decision, on which, though she could never in her wildest dreams have known it, would hang the fate of the entire Hebrew race.

Jochebed was Moses' mother. She already had a son, Aaron, and a daughter, Miriam, when the new Pharaoh, alarmed at the rapid increase of the Israelite slave population, decreed that the midwives should kill all Hebrew males at birth. When this plan failed, he ordered all Egyptians to throw newborn Israelite boys into the crocodile-infested Nile.

We can imagine Jochebed's anxiety about the fate of her unborn baby, which proved to be a boy, but she somehow managed to hide him for three months. Perhaps she spent that time thinking and praying for inspiration. Finally, she got a papyrus basket, waterproofed it with tar (there's the common sense), and placed it among the reeds by the river's edge (there's the faith). Did she know that Pharaoh's daughter bathed there regularly, or did God intervene in direct response to Jochebed's faith, to draw the princess's attention to the basket?

Jochebed also exercised faith, in leaving Miriam watching to see what would happen: even the most reliable children can act unpredictably in moments of great excitement or stress. Again, Jochebed's faith and common sense were rewarded: Miriam came up trumps, innocently offering to find a wet-nurse for the bawling Hebrew infant who had touched the princess's heart. When the princess agreed, Miriam fetched Jochebed, who received her baby back from the jaws of death and was paid to nurse him during his early years.

Jochebed exercised both her common sense in weaving her basket and her faith in leaving it among the reeds. In bringing up our children, neither common sense nor faith alone is enough: we need both. Bring to God today any decision you have to make about your child's upbringing. We can't expect writing in the sky, but I know from my own experience that God does indeed answer our prayers in such circumstances.

Lord, when I have to make important decisions about my children, help me both to 'get the basket' and then to 'leave it by the river'. As my children grow up, help me to grow both in faith and wisdom as I see you working things out for us as a family. Amen.

EXODUS 1:22 – 2:10

7 GOD USES UNLIKELY PEOPLE: RAHAB

'By faith the prostitute Rahab ... was not killed... ' Hebrews 11:31

A couple of years ago, one of our daughters had to spend a year in France. She was sent to the middle of nowhere to teach in a vast, impersonal, concrete edifice resembling a Russian prison, and was desperately lonely and unhappy for the first few weeks. We prayed hard that someone would befriend her. Then two families took her under their wing, welcoming her into their homes, taking her to weddings, on holiday, and generally treating her as a daughter. At the end of the year, we met the families concerned, and I learned an important lesson: God uses the most unlikely people! The French families were not people we would instinctively have been drawn to – they were certainly not practising Christians – but they were undoubtedly God's answer to our fervent prayers for Helen.

At first sight, Rahab seems an unlikely candidate for a place in the family tree of the Lord Jesus Christ. She wasn't an Israelite and she was a prostitute living in the completely pagan city of Jericho. Yet she gets an honourable mention in the chapter of Hebrews which lists heroes and heroines of faith. Why? Because God, in his grace and wisdom, revealed himself to Rahab, and she responded in faith to what she understood of this God who was so much greater than the Canaanite deities around there. She bore witness to that faith, hiding the Israelite spies in return for the promise that she and her family would be spared when Jericho fell to

Joshua's army, which she knew it would. That promise was kept: though everything and everyone else in Jericho was destroyed, Rahab and her family were unharmed. She became the mother of Boaz, and the great-grandmother of King David, an ancestor of Jesus.

God uses the most unlikely people, not just the 'nice', respectable ones with a certain standing in the community, but those who are marginalised, unimportant, even despised. 'God chose the foolish things of the world to shame the wise; God chose the weak things of the world to shame the strong.

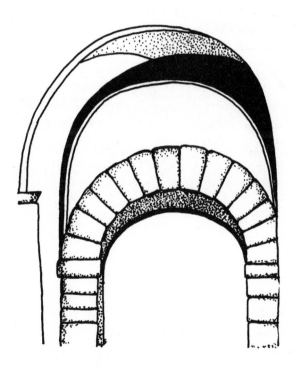

He chose the lowly things of this world and the despised things – and the things that are not – to nullify the things that are, so that no-one may boast before him' (1 Corinthians 1:27–29).

Lord, thank you that no one is beyond the reach of your love and grace, no one too insignificant for you to use. Help me not to pray with blinkers on. Open wide the eyes of my faith so that I can see you at work in the most unlikely people, using them to further your kingdom. And when I feel inadequate, especially about ...., help me to hold on to the fact that you can and do use unlikely candidates! Amen.

Pray for those who are working with people our society tends to marginalise – the drop-outs, the homeless, the inadequate, the handicapped, criminals – and thank God that Jesus came to bring good news to 'the poor' in every sense.

JOSHUA 6:20–25

8 PHYSICALLY BARREN, SPIRITUALLY FERTILE: MANOAH'S WIFE

'The angel of God came ... to the woman while she was out in the field... ' Judges 13:9

Someone once said that we can either look at God through our problems, or at our problems through God.

Do you ever feel anonymous, insignificant, or overwhelmed by a problem? Women seem to find it much more difficult to 'compartmentalise' their lives than men do, and it's easy to allow worries to overshadow everything so that we don't hear or recognise God's voice. Manoah's wife, whose name we don't even know, had a problem – she was childless. In her culture this was regarded as shameful, but she did not allow this fact so to dominate her thinking that she became spiritually insensitive – quite the reverse in fact.

Visited by 'a man of God' or 'the angel of the Lord' – a term often used in the Old Testament for a visit from God himself – Manoah's wife took in all he said about the son she would bear, relaying it back pretty much word for word to her husband. She was aware that this was no ordinary visitor: for her he was 'awesome'; so much so, she did not ask his name (though her husband did!).

Manoah prayed for a second visit (did he think his wife was imagining things?) and the messenger returned, again to Manoah's wife, who had to fetch her husband. The couple then offered the 'man' a meal and were directed instead to offer a burnt offering, in the flame of which the angel of the

Lord ascended to heaven. Manoah panicked, thinking that he and his wife would die, but she calmly told him not to be foolish: why would God go to the trouble of sending the messenger twice if he was intending to kill them? In due course, the promised son, Samson, was born. The Lord blessed him, the Spirit of God came upon him, and he became one of the great judges of Israel.

I think mums can be very encouraged by this rather mysterious story. First, in a culture where women were regarded as mere chattels, the messenger came to Manoah's wife. God regarded her as significant and spiritually sensitive enough to hear and recognise his message.

Second, when the 'man of God' returned, he came to the woman *in the field* – that is, as she was going about her daily tasks. Although it's good to take time out with God if we can, God can and does speak to us 'where we're at', if we stay tuned to him, even when we are frantically busy with children and housework. And we don't need to be problem-free before he does so! I remember occasions when God spoke to me clearly about things that were very much on my mind, occasions when I wasn't in church or even praying, but doing routine things. Busyness doesn't mean God can't speak to us – he can. But we need to be listening!

Lord, thank you that, however anonymous and insignificant I feel, I'm of value to you. Help me to 'stay tuned' to you today, and to recognise your answers – however they come – to the things that I'm concerned about. Amen.

JUDGES 13

9 A MODEL DAUGHTER-IN-LAW: RUTH

'Ruth was determined to go with her... ' Ruth 1:18

I have been very blessed in having in-laws who accepted me right from the start and who never attempted to interfere with the way we led our lives or brought up our family. Not everyone is so blessed. How well do you get on with your in-laws? Here's an ideal to aspire to!

Ruth and Orpah, Moabite women, were married to Israelite brothers who had fled famine in their own country to come to Moab with their parents, Elimelech and Naomi. Father and sons died, leaving the three women behind. A grieving Naomi, hearing that the famine had ended, decided to return to her home town in Judah. Her two daughters-in-law set out with her, but, along the way, Naomi blessed the two younger women and urged them to return to their own families so that they could make second marriages. At first they wouldn't hear of it, but when pressed, Orpah kissed Naomi goodbye and turned back to Moab. Ruth, however, refused to leave, identifying herself completely with the God of Israel and with her mother-in-law.

You are probably familiar with the rest of the story. After a series of God-ordained 'coincidences', Ruth found fulfilment in a second marriage and a son who not only took away Naomi's bitterness but was also the grandfather of King David and an ancestor of Jesus.

What does the book of Ruth have to say to us today? First, I think, it reminds us of the largely-ignored power of blessing others in God's name: there are several examples here and elsewhere in the Old Testament. We can 'bless' our children. For example: Rebekah's brothers blesses her (Gen 24:60), Jacob blessed Pharoah (Gen 47:10) and Joshua blessed Caleb (Joshua 14:13). Second, even allowing for a very different culture, Ruth's actions are a shining example of relationship-building! She was prepared to go back with

Naomi, a self-confessed bitter, empty woman, to a foreign country, with no prospect of remarrying, as Naomi herself warned. Why did Ruth do it? Because she was prepared to put an older woman's welfare before her own and to trust God with the consequences. And God blessed her beyond anything she could have hoped or dreamed.

Do your relationships within your wider family honour God? Are you setting a good example to your children by your attitude to your parents and your parents-in-law? Do you still honour them? Admittedly, our parents' generation can be difficult – but so can we! Ruth had every reason *not* to go with Naomi: she wasn't a blood relation, was of a different race and religion, and was returning to a foreign country where Ruth would be an alien. But Ruth went – and God honoured her.

Lord, I bring to you my relationships within my wider family. Show me how I can improve them. Help me to show love to the more difficult members and to trust you with the outcome. Don't let me bear grudges. Amen.

Pray for people who have problems with their mother-in-law or daughter-in-law.

RUTH 1:1–22

10 BEAUTY FOR ASHES: NAOMI

'He has sent me to ... bestow ... beauty instead of ashes ... gladness instead of mourning and ... praise instead of... despair.' Isaiah 61:1,3

It seemed such a good idea at the time, nipping over the border into Moab to escape the famine. Mahlon and Kilion treated it like a holiday. We settled easily – life wasn't so different in Moab. We had each other for company and quickly got to know the neighbours. Soon it felt as if we'd lived there all our lives.

Then Elimelech died. I was devastated. I wanted to go home, back to my family in Bethlehem. But my sons wanted to stay. I don't blame them – they could barely remember the old life, and there were Moabite girls they were desperate to marry. So there was nothing I could do. I know we're not supposed to marry outside Israel, but there were no Israelite girls around.

I hoped that soon there would be grandchildren, but I was disappointed. As if taking my husband wasn't enough, the Almighty took my sons too. I was left a widow without children or grandchildren. If it hadn't been for my daughters-in-law, I don't know what I'd have done. I know there's talk about 'no-good Moabite women', but speak as you find, I always say. These two were good to me – treated me like their own mother. So perhaps the Almighty hadn't crossed me off his list altogether.

I was miserable, though: I wished we'd stuck it out in Bethlehem. Then word came that the famine there was over, and I just knew that all I wanted to do was go home. The girls said they'd see me to the border, but, when we got there, Orpah took some persuading to go back. Ruth just refused point-blank to leave me – said she'd stick by me whatever, and even worship my God, the God of Abraham. I couldn't convince her otherwise, but I have to admit I was relieved. I was a bit nervous about facing everyone back home again.

When we arrived, there was quite a kerfuffle. I knew I'd probably aged a bit, but people weren't even sure it was me. I always had a reputation for laughing, you see – but what was there to laugh about now? Talk about coming home empty-handed... And, yes, I admit it – I was very bitter. I even called myself Mara, which means bitter, instead of Naomi, which means pleasant.

Ruth, bless her, just quietly got on with providing for me; no fuss, just did as I advised – because, of course, she didn't really know our ways then. And the Almighty definitely hadn't crossed *her* off his list! Oh no... It's a long story, but she married Boaz, one of my husband's family – he's rich *and* good, so she did well for herself there. And so did I, because in no time at all Ruth and Boaz produced this little fellow, my first grandson. Isn't he lovely? And you know what? He's the spit of my Elimelech.

Lord, show me where you want to give me beauty instead of ashes, and joy instead of mourning. Amen.

RUTH 4:13–17

11 A SON ON LOAN FROM GOD: HANNAH

'I prayed for this child ...
Now I give him to the Lord.' 1 Samuel 1:27–28

Some friends of ours recently adopted a son. It's been wonderful to see and share their joy after the years of childlessness and longing for a family.

Like several other women in these reflections, Hannah was childless – as great a sadness then as now; but also, in that culture, a disgrace. To make matters worse, Hannah's husband had another wife, Peninnah, who did have children.

Here is another vivid picture of domestic tension. We are told twice that Elkanah loved Hannah: so perhaps he only married Peninnah because Hannah couldn't have children. Maybe Peninnah resented the fact that Hannah was greatly loved, because she 'kept provoking her in order to irritate her. This went on year after year'.

The whole family regularly went up to the sanctuary at Shiloh, to sacrifice and worship God there. Whenever they went, Peninnah would provoke Hannah 'till she wept and would not eat'. Evidently, Hannah didn't complain to her husband about Peninnah's superior attitude and constant jibing, because Elkanah seems completely at a loss to understand the source of Hannah's grief. Hannah handled it by allowing herself to weep – almost always a good move! – and by pouring out her distress to God – another good move! She prayed, asking God for a son and vowing that she would 'give him to the Lord for all the days of his life'.

This was the state of distress Hannah was in when she encountered Eli, the priest. Adding insult to injury, he reprimanded her for being drunk. But Hannah protested, explaining, 'I have been praying here out of my great anguish and grief.' Eli's response was gracious: 'Go in peace, and may the God of Israel grant you what you have asked of him.'

And God answered. Hannah had a son, Samuel, who remained at home with her until he was weaned (probably at around three or four years in those days). Then, keeping her promise, Hannah took him to Shiloh and handed him over

to be brought up in God's house. What a wrench that must have been! But Hannah was acknowledging publicly something that all mothers need to see – 'our' children are 'on loan' to us from God and one day we will be required to give an account of how we brought them up. It's an awesome thought.

It's also very comforting – for if our children are on loan to us from God, then he is more concerned for them even than we are.

God gave Hannah five more children, but she never forgot her small son growing up far from home: 'Each year his mother made him a little robe and took it to him when she went up with her husband to offer the annual sacrifice.' And the little boy growing up in the shadow of the ark of the Covenant became Samuel, one of the great prophets of Israel.

Lord, help me to acknowledge, and to remember, that 'my' children are on loan from you. Thank you that you are more concerned for their welfare than I am. Help me to let them 'go with God' at the appropriate time. Amen.

Pray for women whose husbands seem insensitive to their emotional needs.

1 SAMUEL 1

12 ENDURING MOTHER-LOVE: RIZPAH

*'Rizpah ... took sackcloth and spread it
out for herself on a rock.'* 2 Samuel 21:10

'Many waters cannot quench love; rivers cannot wash it
away' (Song of Songs 8:7).

Are there any lengths to which mothers won't go for
their children?

Israel was going through a severe famine. The previous
king, Saul, had apparently brought this upon the country by
his acts of genocide against the Gibeonites who had a long-
standing 'special relationship' with Israel. Anxious to bring the
famine to an end, King David asked the survivors how he
could put matters right. Their request? That seven male
descendants of Saul be put to death. Then the famine would
end. It's hard for us to get our heads round this, isn't it?

Five of Saul's grandsons and his two sons by Rizpah, who
was 'just' a concubine, were executed and their bodies
exposed on a hillside. We can only begin to imagine
Rizpah's grief at seeing her sons put to death for their father's
crimes. Her instinctive reaction might have been to
withdraw and mourn privately. Instead, her fierce maternal
instinct came to the fore and she kept vigil over the bodies
of those young men whom she had probably watched
growing up. Her presence prevented predators from
devouring the corpses, but it must have been a terrible ordeal
for her, lasting up to six months, 'from the beginning of the
harvest till the rain poured down from the heavens'.

Rizpah's actions were reported to David. He was so moved that he took the seven young men's bones and buried them, along with the bones of his best friend Jonathan, Saul's son, and of Saul himself, taken from the place where they'd been hastily interred after their deaths in battle. Rizpah's devotion had touched the king's heart and caused him to act.

We know in our heads that once those young men had died, it made no difference what happened to their bodies. Nevertheless, we – like David – can be deeply moved by Rizpah's long vigil, springing from a mother's love.

We can never give our children too much of this kind of deep devotion, the pouring out of ourselves for their welfare, the sacrificial love which comes from a mother's heart and which endures even after death. This love is a reflection of God's deep, sacrificial love for each of us, his children, so we can be sure he understands the fierce, protective love we feel for ours, an emotion unlike anything else! We can bring to God our concerns for them, knowing that our loving prayers can move him to action on their behalf, just as Rizpah's devotion moved King David.

Lord, you understand the fierce, protective love I feel for .... You know my concerns for him/her, especially .... Give me wisdom to do what I can and to leave the rest with you. Amen.

Reach out now in prayer, bringing before God the needs of mothers who are desperate or who have lost children.

2 SAMUEL 21:1–14

13 PLEADING ON OUR CHILDREN'S BEHALF: BATHSHEBA

'The Lord is faithful to all his promises ...
He fulfils the desires of those who fear him ...' Psalm 145:13,19

A few years ago one of our teenagers refused point-blank to come to church any more. She wrote a note explaining that she still loved us but had decided Christianity was not for her. I was devastated, until I remembered that this child's birth had been pretty dramatic. She nearly died when I was in the last stages of labour, and was finally delivered, not a moment too soon, by emergency Caesarean. She could easily have been stillborn or brain-damaged. After considering this, I said to myself, 'God didn't allow her to survive just to be a spiritual casualty,' and then to God, 'I'll do anything if it helps bring her back to you.'

Shortly afterwards, she asked if a homeless friend of hers could stay with us. With some misgivings and after long discussions and prayer, my husband and I agreed. It was a very difficult time. The young man concerned abused our hospitality and became increasingly hostile, even to the daughter who had asked us to have him. When he finally left, she said, 'You were right, Mum. I'm sorry.' – two things teenagers find it very hard to say! From then on she gradually regained her interest in spiritual things.

As you read this, you may be facing the sadness of seeing children turning away from Christian values. Nagging doesn't help, so what can we do?

I think the story of Bathsheba can give us some ideas. King David, now old and frail, seems to have kept to his room and not had much grip on what was happening in the kingdom. He had several wives and concubines, so his family comprised a number of half-siblings. Assuming his father was 'past it', Adonijah, his eldest living son, announced that he would be king and set arrangements in motion.

The prophet Nathan warned Bathsheba, David's wife and Solomon's mother, that if Adonijah became king, her life and Solomon's would be at risk. Nathan advised her to plead with David for Solomon to succeed him. This she did, reminding David of the oath he had already sworn, that Solomon would be king after him. David's response was quickly to have Solomon crowned king, thus averting disaster.

In the same way that Bathsheba pleaded with David on her son's behalf, I believe, we can plead with God on behalf of our children, especially those who seem to be losing their way

spiritually. God has promised to honour those who honour him. As we remind him of the promises we made when our children were small, perhaps at their baptism or dedication, we can ask, humbly but in faith, for the fulfilment of these promises and for those children to be brought back to him and to the spiritual inheritance that is their right.

Lord, I humbly remind you of the promises we made for .... Please renew his/her faith in you. Amen.

Pray for teenagers you know who seem to have lost their way spiritually, and for parents in distress over teenagers.

1 KINGS 1:28–40

14 GOD USES PEOPLE WITH FEW RESOURCES: THE WIDOW OF ZAREPHATH

'Give, and it will be given to you.' Luke 6:38

Elijah? Yes, I knew him. He stayed with us for a while during the great drought. He wasn't an easy man, mind you – he could be outspoken and moody – but he was straightforward. You knew where you were with him.

I'm not an Israelite, but I realised, after my husband died, that the Israelites' God was better than all ours put together; so I tried to worship him. I didn't know much about it, though – not before Elijah came.

I'd heard of Elijah before I met him. News of his first run-in with Ahab (now *he* was a nasty piece of work) travelled fast. One day I just had this feeling that Elijah was coming and that I should offer him something to eat. I can't describe it any better than that – you know how sometimes you just know something? Perhaps it was God (the God of Israel, I mean) telling me – I don't know. But why would God bother with me?

Anyway, sure enough, while I'm picking up sticks – and there were plenty of them, with the drought – I look up and see this man coming towards me. I guessed it was Elijah because he looked just like a prophet – all hair and beard, and flowing cloak and stick. It was a hot day and he said, 'Would you be so kind as to bring me a drink of water?' I knew then that I hadn't imagined my earlier feeling. But what was I going to give him to eat?

As I'm going to get the water, he calls out, 'And could you spare a piece of bread?' So I told him: 'I don't have anything to spare, God knows! All I've got left is a handful of flour and some oil. I was collecting these sticks to make one last loaf for myself and my son, and then...' I shrugged, wondering what the great prophet would make of that.

He was surprisingly gentle, though I must have sounded a bit rude. 'Go home and make your bread,' he says, 'but make me a little first. Because God says that your flour and oil won't run out until the drought is over!' Well, that took some swallowing, but I decided I had nothing to lose. If we were going to die of starvation, giving the prophet a bit of our last loaf wasn't going to hasten the process too much, was it?

Of course, Elijah was right! And so was I, about his God being better than all the rest put together. The flour and the oil lasted till the drought ended.

Lord, you used a poor widow to meet Elijah's needs, and you met her needs as she obeyed you. Show me how, even with my limited resources, I can bless others and be blessed in return. Amen.

1 KINGS 17:7–16

15 GOD MEETS MATERIAL NEEDS: THE WIDOW'S OIL

'... my God will meet all your needs...' Philippians 4:19

When I was four years old, I learned that God is interested in the details of our lives and that he answers prayer. We lived, in the early 1950s, in a remote Essex village, with one bus three times a week to and from the nearest town. One day, my mother took me on the bus to the dentist. Food rationing was still in force after World War II and goods not seen for years were reappearing in the shops. I saw something interesting in a greengrocer's and asked what it was. My mother told me it was a coconut. I asked if I could have one. She explained that she didn't have the money to buy it for me, adding that I would have to 'ask Jesus' to send me one. I didn't forget, and at bedtime that night I prayed for a coconut.

The next day, the postman delivered a package from my mother's aunt in Gloucestershire, who sent us parcels occasionally. Inside, along with the usual jellies, custard powder and good quality hand-me-downs from the wealthy family she worked for, was – a coconut! She had never before sent a coconut and she never sent one again. There was no way she could have known I'd prayed for one – neither she nor we had a telephone. She wasn't even a Christian, but God used her to answer my prayer!

God can and does meet material, practical, spiritual and emotional needs, as we can see from the story of the widow left to cope with her husband's debts. She asked the prophet Elisha how she could prevent her sons being taken as slaves by her husband's creditors. All she had left was a little oil. The prophet told her to borrow lots of jars ('Don't ask for just a few') and to start filling them with oil. The oil lasted and lasted, until all the jars were full – a reminder that God gives to us sometimes according to our faith and obedience! The widow sold the oil and repaid the debt.

Often the practical necessity of making ends meet in a household falls on the mother. The responsibility of stretching the money available for food and things like school uniform is yours. God is interested in that. He can and does answer prayer for practical necessities. Why not ask him?

Lord, you know I'm finding it hard to make ends meet. Please show me what to do, and meet our needs. Amen.

Reach out in prayer for families in developing countries who have had to sell even their young children to factory owners to help the family income.

2 KINGS 4:1–7

16 TAKING THE SPIRITUAL INITIATIVE: THE WOMAN FROM SHUNEM

'We have different gifts, according to the grace given us.' Romans 12:6

When my children were small, I had lots of ideas about how we could use family prayer times. However, I was unsure about suggesting them because I thought that, since my husband was the head of the family, all spiritual leadership should come from him – an idea which teaching at the time in some parts of the church did nothing to dispel. But my husband's gifts lie in completely different areas from mine. I finally learned that it was OK to use the gifts God had given to me, wherever and however he showed me. God speaks directly to us as women, even if we have capable, godly husbands. His gifts in you are to be nurtured and used, not quenched or hidden.

Here is another story of a mother who used her initiative and wouldn't let anything prevent her from getting help for her child. This woman, who appears not to have been an Israelite, fell into the habit of offering Elisha a meal whenever he visited her village. She was sensitive enough spiritually to realise that he was God's messenger, and suggested to her husband that they build a small guest-room on their roof for the prophet.

Elisha wanted to repay her thoughtfulness and asked if anything could be done for her. It's possible that she spoke a different language, as Gehazi, Elisha's servant, seems to have acted as interpreter; and it's possible that suggesting she could do with a son was Gehazi's idea!

When she was told she would have a son the woman could hardly take it in, but the following year she gave birth to him. However, tragedy struck – when the child was a little older, he became seriously ill with sunstroke and died.

The woman acted at once, concealing the bad news from her elderly husband and setting out immediately to fetch Elisha. Refusing to be fobbed off by Gehazi, she challenged the prophet – she hadn't even asked for a son and now God had taken him! She would not leave until Elisha went with her, and God used Elisha to restore her son to life.

Undue emphasis in certain parts of the church on women being 'submissive' can lead to a situation where they become paralysed spiritually, afraid to make suggestions or act on their own initiative. The Shunammite woman was confident enough first to recognise Elisha as a man of God, then to suggest to her husband that they build him a room. When her son died, she was composed enough to hide her distress and the bad news from her husband while she went to the only person she knew who might be able to help. God rewarded her faith and her initiative.

Lord, show me if there are gifts I'm not using because of fear or misunderstanding. Help me to use them in my family, even if I can't at present use them elsewhere. Amen.

2 KINGS 4:8–37

17 AUNTS CAN MAKE A DIFFERENCE: JEHOSHEBA

'She did what she could.' Mark 14:8

Have you noticed how children sometimes resemble their aunts and uncles more than their parents? My sister and youngest brother often say to me (not always approvingly!) about their respective daughters, 'She's just like you!' I can see that these particular nieces (I have nine altogether) are very like me in some ways, and this has encouraged good relationships with them in areas where we are on the same wavelength. Children who grow up enjoying their extended families are indeed blessed, and aunts and uncles can make a very significant contribution, as the story of Jehosheba reminds us.

Old Testament kings were constantly being killed and replaced. The Bible relates how, once King Ahaziah was dead, his evil mother, Athaliah, started systematically destroying his family in order to reign herself. However, Jehosheba, a sister of the late king and married to Jehoiada the high priest, managed to rescue her nephew, the infant prince Joash, and hide him and his nurse in a 'bedroom' (probably a storeroom for couches and mattresses) for six years. Then Joash was crowned king and 'did what was right in the eyes of the Lord all the years of Jehoiada the priest'.

Jehosheba must have been faced with an awful dilemma. She may well have risked her own life in snatching this little boy 'from among the royal princes... about to be murdered'. She almost certainly agonised, as any of us would, over the fact that it would clearly be impossible to save them all. It must have been heartbreaking that she could only rescue one. But she did make a difference to the life of that one – and he became, at least initially, a good king after a succession of thoroughly bad ones.

What truths are there for us in this account? First, aunts are important! If you're not a mum but you are an aunt, then be encouraged – you can make a difference in the lives of your nieces and nephews. Second, we all have to accept that

we are only human and can never meet everyone's needs. In choosing to help one person or one charity, we are almost inevitably choosing *not* to help another, equally deserving, one. Women seem to find this more difficult than men, but if we can't accept our limitations we will drive ourselves insane by worrying about what we can't do.

Finally, when we bring God into the equation, and act in faith and obedience to him, we may be setting in motion something of immense significance. In the Gospels, Jesus commented of one woman, 'She did what she could' (Mark 14:8). That is all God asks of us.

Thank God for relatives who have made a difference to you, and ask him to show you if there's anyone for whom you can make a difference, even if it's 'only' by praying. Amen.

Pray for people such as aid workers and missionaries, who have limited resources but work in areas of great need, unable to help all who need help, and being forced to prioritise. Ask that they may be given godly wisdom in all their decision-making, and freedom from guilt about those they have not been able to assist.

2 CHRONICLES 22:10–12; 24:1–2

18 THE TWENTY-FIRST CENTURY SUPERMUM

'A kind-hearted woman gains respect...' Proverbs 11:16

The book of Proverbs contains several references to children learning from their mothers. I wanted to include something on the famous passage in the final chapter, about the ideal wife and mother, but really the passage itself says it all. What follows is a paraphrase. If, after reading it, you feel you still have a long way to go – join the club!

> What makes a great wife and mum? She's hard to
>   find these days!
> Her husband trusts her completely, and she enriches
>   his life,
> supporting him and never undermining him.
>
> Costumes for the school play? She's happy to help –
> knows just where to get the stuff they need,
> and stays up very late (again!) making them.
>
> She's organised about her food shopping,
> recycles as much as possible, does a part-time job,
> and grows what she can in the garden.
>
> This woman makes sure she stays fit and healthy,
> keeps an eye on where the money goes –
> and never forgets to take the bread out of the freezer!

She always has some project in hand,
is generous and enthusiastic to a fault
and concerned for Fair Trade and the world's poor.

She doesn't worry when winter arrives because
she gently reminded her husband (twice) a few
    months ago
to check that the central heating was working.

She puts her practical gifts to good use
in making a comfortable home
and contributing to the family income.

She dresses well, without ostentation,
and her husband is held in respect
in the church and the community.

She has presence and an inner strength,
facing the future, whatever it may hold,
with calm – and a sense of humour.

She never gives advice unasked,
but is known for her wisdom and common sense
and can be relied on for an honest opinion.

She is always busy, never idle,
keeping track of everyone and everything
so that family life runs smoothly.

She can find geometry sets and football boots,
remembers to record that important TV programme,
and writes regularly to her children at university.

Her family finally appreciate her,
recognising all she has done for them;
they tell her she's great – and mean it!

Her husband actually puts it into words too –
'Lots of women have busy, useful lives,
but you are the best and I love you.'

Charm is superficial, and beauty skin-deep,
but the woman who honours God in her family life
will have something more lasting – an eternal reward.

Lord, I'd like to be like this, but I can't do it on my own! Please help me. Thank you that you love me and accept me anyway, just as I am: untidy, disorganised... (supply own adjectives!), and even if I never manage to be a 'supermum', help me and the family to have fun along the way. Amen.

PROVERBS 31:10–31

19 GOD'S MOTHER-HEART 1

'Like a woman in childbirth I cry out,
I gasp and pant.' Isaiah 42:14

The Bible always refers to God as 'he', but this doesn't mean that God is male! According to Genesis, man and woman were both made in God's image, so God, who is spirit, must possess characteristics which we think of as female and some we think of as male.

Does this really matter? In some ways, no, because we can never really know God by words alone. However, in some ways and for some people, I believe it matters a lot. First, for people whose own fathers have been absent, abusive or less than ideal, the thought that God can be a mother as well as a father may be positive and helpful. Second, when we become mothers, we gradually become conscious of a range of protective emotions and reactions towards our children of which we were previously unaware. These feelings can, I believe, actually help us understand more clearly God's love for, and delight in, us, and thus deepen our relationship with him.

I hope you will see what I mean as we look at some Bible passages in which God displays characteristics that we think of as motherly rather than fatherly.

Isaiah 49:15 says, 'Can a woman forget the baby at her breast and have no compassion on the child she has borne? Though she may forget, I will not forget you!' This description will immediately strike a chord with most mothers who have breastfed a new baby. It is physically impossible to forget a breastfeeding child, because you are aware, all the time, of lactating. The cry of *any* baby, not just your own, will trigger a physical sensation in the breast and a spurt of milk. It is as if God is giving a double reassurance: 'Even if it were possible – *which it isn't* – for a mother to forget her breastfeeding infant, I will never, ever forget you.'

And we will also immediately identify with the feelings of tender intimacy and intense, loving protectiveness that a mother feels towards her nursing child.

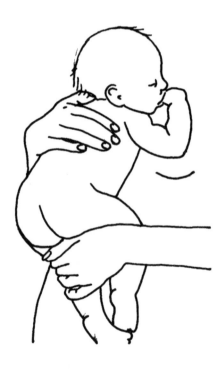

Isaiah 66:11–13 describes Jerusalem as a nursing mother: those who love her 'will nurse and be satisfied at her comforting breasts ... carried on her arm and dandled on her knees ... As a mother comforts her child, so will I comfort you ...' Once again, the imagery used is obviously maternal and speaks particularly to mothers as we respond with our hearts as well as with our heads to what God is saying. We gain a better understanding of God's feelings for us, because it taps into our own experience as mothers – we know how we feel when we comfort our own children.

Lord, open my heart to receive and to respond to the motherly tenderness and comfort you long to give. Amen.

Pray for people who have been damaged by their own fathers, and therefore find the idea of God as Father a difficult or repellent one. Ask that they may be able to respond to God's tender mother-love instead.

ISAIAH 49:15; 66:11–13

20 GOD'S MOTHER-HEART 2

'I have loved you with an everlasting love...' Jeremiah 31:3

I reflected earlier on two passages in the Bible which suggest to us that God has a mother-heart. I'd like to consider this a little further.

Deuteronomy 32:11 is part of the Song of Moses, a long poem describing God's relationship with his chosen people: '...like an eagle that stirs up its nest and hovers over its young, that spreads its wings to catch them and carries them on its pinions'. The mother eagle disturbs her nest to get her fledglings out over the edge, thus ensuring that they attempt to fly. When she sees that the youngsters are tired or in danger of crash-landing, she swoops down and catches them on her own powerful wings.

Here is a lovely view of God as a mother bird which instinctively keeps the right balance between encouraging young ones to strike out alone and rescuing them when the situation is too much for their lack of strength or experience. It's as if God is saying, 'Like the mother eagle, I may stir up your nest so that you stretch your wings and learn to fly. But I'm also there to catch and support you if things get tough.'

In the New Testament, Matthew 23:37 gives us a brief glimpse into the 'mother-heart' of Jesus. This picture comes after a long catalogue of 'Woes' during which Jesus roundly condemns hypocrisy and double-dealing. Suddenly, the mood changes to that of compassionate yearning: 'O

Jerusalem … how often I have longed to gather your children together, as a hen gathers her chicks under her wings, but you were not willing.' In his parables Jesus often used familiar everyday scenes to catch his listeners' attention, and this image is made more striking by its very ordinariness – a hen covering her chicks with her wings to provide them with warmth and safety. Jesus wanted so much to take Jerusalem under his wings. The picture expresses vividly his warmth and compassion for those around him.

If we appreciate and respond to God's 'maternal' feelings for us, his children, and realise that he understands perfectly our feelings as mothers for our own children, we can feel free to bring to his mother-heart any concerns we may have for them.

Lord, I thank you for these pictures in your word which reveal to me your loving mother-heart. Help me to respond to your love as I want my children to respond to mine. Teach me to love them with the tenderness and patience that you show me. Amen.

DEUTERONOMY 32:11; MATTHEW 23:37

21 RACHEL WEEPS

'My soul is in anguish.
How long, O Lord, how long?'
Psalm 6:3

Losing a child must be every parent's worst nightmare. Television and the newspapers are full of the images of war and children suffering as a result. I was reminded of this when I read the story of Herod's slaughter of all boys under two in Bethlehem, after the visit of the wise men. Rachel is every mother who has ever lost a child to violence.

A voice is heard in Ramah...
Rachel weeping for her children,
and refusing to be comforted
because they are no more.

In Sierra Leone, Kosovo, Chechnya...
Rachel weeps still,
refusing all comfort.
Her children are no more.

Still, Herods burn with bloodlust;
still, innocence is slaughtered.
Murdered by madmen,
Rachel's children are no more.

Down the years, so many Rachels
with but one voice –
mothers drowning in grief for
their children who are no more.

Frail flames snuffed out at a
tyrant's whim or despot's decree.
Rachel cries, 'No more!
How long, O Lord, how long?

'How long will men beat
their ploughshares into swords,
their pruning-hooks to spears –
till there are no more children?'

Rachel weeping...
Why do you weep?
refusing to be comforted...
The God of all comfort.
for her children...
Let the little children come to me!
who are no more.
They shine as the sun in the kingdom of their Father.

Pray for mothers the world over who have lost children through violence or warfare, and for those seeking to be peacemakers.

MATTHEW 2:16–18

22 PUSHY MOTHERS: ZEBEDEE'S WIFE

'...humility comes before honour.' Proverbs 18:12

Pushy mothers: we have all met them and cringed. They either think their offspring have a right to star in everything from sports day to the nativity play; or they push the poor children (academically or in extra-curricular activities) beyond what those children are capable of or want. Often this behaviour seems to spring from a desire to have their children achieve what they themselves never managed.

Pushy mothers are clearly not a new breed. In Matthew's Gospel, the mother of James and John came to Jesus, wanting to reserve seats at the top table, as it were, for her sons in the kingdom of God. I must confess that the incident, though serious, makes me smile: James's, and John's, nickname was – 'Sons of Thunder' they clearly didn't have a problem with assertiveness and probably didn't need their mother to put in a word for them!

The sad thing is that Zebedee's wife obviously had some spiritual awareness: she latched on to the concept of Jesus' kingdom and clearly believed in it, although it's possible she was expecting him to found an earthly kingdom. She knelt down to ask the favour, so outwardly she was submitting to Jesus' authority. But, as Jesus pointed out, neither James nor John nor their mother, nor indeed the rest of the disciples – really understood what God's kingdom was about – being a servant, putting others first, and facing likely suffering and death.

We would hate to think of ourselves as pushy, but we can all be tempted that way. Of course, we need to build up our children's self-esteem, and it's absolutely right that we should think our children are wonderful and tell them so. However, wanting them to be 'stars', and pushing for it, cuts right across Jesus' teaching here. It is a more valuable lesson for our children to learn to do their best in the back row of the chorus, than to be grouchy and moody because they didn't get the star role. We do them no favours by suggesting that they should always have the plum parts – even in a church production! A little humility still goes a long way!

Lord, you know I want the best for my children, but help me to show them that what we want isn't necessarily your best. Help me to encourage my children to pull their weight whatever they are assigned to do, and teach them the value of doing everything as if they are doing it for you. Amen.

Meditate on the fact that in the kingdom of God being a servant is very important! Pray for those who submit outwardly to Jesus' authority, but who still haven't grasped what it means to have a servant-heart.

MATTHEW 20:20–28

23 USING OUR CHILDREN TO ACHIEVE OUR OWN ENDS: HERODIAS

'Train a child in the way (s)he should go...' Proverbs 22:6
'His mother encouraged him in doing ...
evil in the eyes of the Lord...' 2 Chronicles 22:3,4

This horrendous story should serve as an awful warning to any parent tempted to use their children to achieve their own ends. John the Baptist, never one for pussyfooting, had rebuked King Herod for taking his brother's wife, Herodias. Herod, obviously deeply affected by John's remarks, threw John into prison in order to silence him. Herodias, however, was bent on revenge. She bided her time and brooded.

Then, on Herod's birthday, Herodias's daughter danced for the king and his VIP guests. Herod was so pleased with her dancing that, in true fairy-tale fashion, he rashly and publicly promised her whatever she asked for – 'up to half my kingdom'. There all resemblance to a fairy-tale ends. Herodias, seizing her opportunity, instructed her daughter to ask for the head of John the Baptist. The girl brought this terrible request to the king – and Herod was well and truly trapped. John was beheaded, his head given to the girl on a platter, *and the girl gave it to her mother.*

Familiarity with this story has perhaps dulled the sickening horror of it. What effect did receiving that grisly offering have on the young girl? Was she psychologically scarred for life – or just brutalised? Did Herodias herself ever regret her rash words or impetuous revenge? One thing is certain: in this incident we see a complete travesty of the mother–daughter relationship.

How old was the daughter? Old enough to dance in public, but not, apparently, of marriageable age, so she was probably still a teenager. We can imagine her, almost

speechless with excitement at the applause and Herod's breathtaking offer, unable to think straight in the heat of the moment; and rushing to ask her mother what she should say. And the mother, seeing her own advantage, never thinking or caring what effect it might have on her child, made her not just an accessory to cold-blooded murder but a witness to its aftermath.

Have you ever caught yourself using your child or children for your own ends? We may not be tempted to anything so evil as Herodias, but we do need to beware of using or manipulating our children to get what we want. To betray that relationship of trust so as to gain advantage for ourselves is wrong. Sadly, we sometimes don't realise what we are doing until it is almost too late.

Lord, please show me if there are any ways in which I am trying to use or manipulate my children for my own ends, to achieve my ambition or to fulfil a dream. Give me selfless love for them and help me always to put their welfare before anything else. Amen.

Pray for children and young people who have been abused, and for those let down by their parents or others with a duty of care towards them.

MARK 6:14–29

24 THE DESPERATE MOTHER: THE CANAANITE WOMAN

'Woman, you have great faith! Your request is granted.' Matthew 15:28

I only went because I was desperate – I know what Jews think about us Greeks. 'Dogs' is their politest term. Of course, I'd heard of Jesus. Who hadn't? The Jews had many rabbis, but this one put his money where his mouth was and *did* something to help the poor, the sick and the leprosy sufferers. It was hearing about those with leprosy that gave me the courage to go. If this Jesus would touch someone with leprosy, maybe there was a chance for me – a woman and a Gentile.

My little girl was more than sick. Nobody could do anything with her – she was like a wild animal. Demon-possession is a terrible thing, especially in a young child. I'd tried everything – doctors, sacrifices – but nothing made any difference. It was like having two daughters: one sweet and gentle, the other an unrecognisable savage. I was at the end of my tether. When I heard Jesus was in the area, the thought just popped into my head: *Ask Jesus to heal her.*

Before I could talk myself out of it, I was on my way. It wasn't difficult to find him: Jews don't often come here, and people talk. When I reached the house, his bodyguards, or whatever they call themselves, wouldn't let me in. I could almost read their thoughts: *Who does she think she is?*

I refused to leave. They wouldn't touch me – I was worse than a leper in their eyes – so they couldn't physically remove me. I heard one say, 'Tell Jesus to get rid of her, otherwise she'll plague us all night.' Too right I would. In the end I just pushed past them, threw myself at Jesus' feet and begged him: 'Lord, help me!'

The men said, 'Send her away – she's a nuisance!' How'd they feel if it was *their* child? But Jesus ignored them. He seemed uncertain, almost as if he was waiting for permission. Then he looked right at me. 'First let the children eat all they want, for it is not right to take the children's bread and toss it to their dogs,' he said, but not in a nasty way, almost if he was presenting me with a challenge. Even as he was saying it, I had an answer: 'Yes, Lord, but even the dogs under the table eat the children's crumbs.'

Jesus smiled – I thought he was going to laugh out loud. In that smile I saw something I'd never seen before on anyone's face, as if he knew all about me and loved me – me, a Gentile and a woman! 'For such a reply, you may go,' he said. 'Your daughter is better.'

And, of course, she was. And she's never been troubled since.

Lord, I feel desperate about .... Please bring your healing and peace to the situation. Amen.

Pray for mothers at the end of their tether, especially those whose children have desperate problems.

MARK 7:24–30

25 MOTHERS BRING CHILDREN TO JESUS

'...the kingdom of heaven belongs to such as these.' Matthew 19:14

This incident is recorded in three of the four Gospels, but the most vivid account is in Mark. People were bringing their small children to Jesus for him to bless them, and the disciples told them off. (This makes me think that it was their mothers

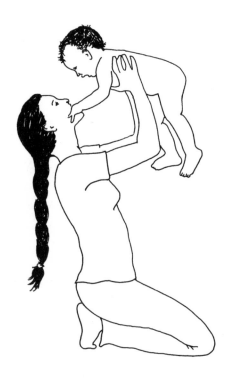

who brought them: perhaps the disciples would have thought twice about rebuking fathers!) When Jesus heard what was happening, he was *indignant*. He was angry that the disciples were preventing children from reaching him, and rebuked them: 'Let the little children come to me, and do not hinder them, for the kingdom of God belongs to such as these.'

Children do not have to be adult to come to faith. Rather, the opposite is true: adults must become like children in their receptiveness, trust and dependence on their heavenly Father if they wish to enter his kingdom. It is wonderful to see young children grow in faith, ready to trust God in situations where we adults are often readier to doubt. Infant prayers frequently provide us with wonderful lessons in how to talk to God!

Jesus, of course, was the eldest of at least six children – we know that he had sisters as well as three brothers. He probably grew up keeping a weather eye on his younger siblings. Eldest children often have a deep love for small children, which Jesus clearly demonstrates here. He so obviously loved children and wanted them to come to him, that we can be confident about bringing our children, from birth onwards, to him in prayer. And, as we experience the joys and sorrows of motherhood, we can perhaps begin to understand better God's parent-love for us.

Lord, help me bring my children to you often. Give me a child's faith and trust in you. Amen.

MARK 10:13–16

26 COPING WITH AN UNPLANNED PREGNANCY: MARY

'I will turn the darkness into light ... and make the rough places smooth.' Isaiah 42:16

Have you ever got up anticipating a run-of-the-mill day and then been surprised by something completely unexpected? This must have been one of those days for Mary!

God sent his angel, Gabriel, to small, obscure Nazareth, to an unknown, probably illiterate teenage girl, to tell her that she was to bear God's son. Mary recognised somehow that this was God's messenger, but she was, understandably, *troubled*.

Why did God choose Mary? I think the clue comes in her response: 'I am the Lord's servant. May it be to me as you have said.' God, who knows us better than we know ourselves, looked at Mary and saw a serving heart. She was willing to do whatever God wanted. Mary wasn't offered any options: she was told that this baby was going to happen. The element of choice lay in her response to the inevitable.

How did Mary feel when Gabriel had gone? Her mind must have been reeling as the implications of his message sank in. What would she tell Joseph? Her parents? What would the neighbours say? So the other information given by Gabriel – that Mary's relative, Elizabeth, was also miraculously pregnant – was, I believe, God's lifeline for Mary as she faced this incredible situation. The older woman would be the ideal person to help her through the turmoil of early pregnancy.

Despite her willingness, Mary sometimes got it wrong in bringing up her son. But God sees the desires of our hearts and honours them when, deep down, we want more than anything to glorify him in our family life. Any pregnancy, but especially one that is unplanned, can throw us into confusion. And sometimes other unexpected family

situations will arise and threaten to overwhelm us emotionally – as I write this, my husband has just been made redundant, completely unexpectedly, for the second time in eight years. But God is never taken by surprise, never thrown into confusion. Nothing can separate us and our children, born or unborn, from his love.

An unexpected pregnancy or other unforeseen circumstances may be shaking your security, but you can *choose* how you respond. If you can say with Mary, 'I am the Lord's servant. May it be to me as you have said,' you will find that God provides for you, as he did for Mary, a lifeline of human encouragement. As you respond positively with faith, God will either see you through the pregnancy, preparing you to mother the child you will bear; or he will carry and comfort you through other unexpected situations, giving you the grace and strength you need to cope.

Lord, I'm in turmoil about the situation I find myself in. Help me, like Mary, to accept it. And help me to trust you to meet my needs, and the needs of everyone else involved, in ways I could never have imagined. Amen.

Reach out in prayer for teenage mums and their children.

LUKE 1:26–45

27 THE ENCOURAGER: ELIZABETH

'...let us encourage one another...' Hebrews 10:25

God-fearing Elizabeth, 'well on in years' but miraculously pregnant, hid herself for five months, before having an unexpected visit from her cousin, Mary, also miraculously pregnant. And what a welcome Mary received! Elizabeth encouraged the younger woman by affirming and blessing her. There is no suggestion that she resented the fact that Mary's child would be greater than the child Elizabeth herself was carrying (John the Baptist); no hint that she felt 'upstaged'. Elizabeth recognised Mary's calling and encouraged her in it.

Mary stayed with Elizabeth for three months – and those first three months of pregnancy can be the worst, can't they? You are tired and frequently feel, and are, sick. It must have been so comforting for Mary to spend that time with a mature woman whom she trusted and who had herself just experienced the early stages of pregnancy. And who better than a respected priest's wife to protect Mary from wagging tongues?

Unfortunately, we see nothing of Elizabeth's mothering of John, though he can't have been an easy child. Elizabeth herself was old enough to be his grandmother, but from this brief insight into her reaction to Mary we can see how wise, sensitive and caring she was. She must have brought those elements of her character to bear on John's upbringing.

Elizabeth – God's lifeline for Mary – is a wonderful example of encouragement. But Mary had had an angelic visit, a message from God himself. Why should she need anything else? Because, like us, Mary was human. God knows that however 'spiritual' we are, we need to be affirmed, especially if we are based at home, caring for babies and small children, often round the clock.

Our children need encouraging, too, so let's take every opportunity to encourage them by affirming and praising them. So often we nag them about the bad things much more than we encourage them about the good ones, even though we know children respond better to praise and encouragement than to nagging and scolding.

Maybe you aren't a mum, or maybe you, like Elizabeth, are older than the young mums you know. They may not want advice they don't ask for, but they *do* need encouragement! Ask God to make you an encourager. Sometimes, sadly, we don't receive from others the encouragement we long for. However, in such circumstances, we can find it in God himself.

God of encouragement, thank you for those who encourage me and for the example of Elizabeth. Show me how I can be an encourager. Help me to be positive with my own children and with others I meet, praising them for the good things, building their self-esteem and not nagging about their failures. Amen.

LUKE 1:5–25,39–45,57–80

28 RECOGNISING SPIRITUAL GROWTH: MARY

'...from infancy you have known the holy Scriptures...' 2 Timothy 3:15

Picture the scene. I'm waiting for the lifts in a crowded department store, with baby number three in the buggy. My five-year-old, biddable as ever, is holding obediently onto the handle. My three-year-old, impatient as ever, is leaping up and down. As the first lift arrives and the automatic doors open, I see at a glance that there is not room for all four of us and the buggy. The three-year-old doesn't, however. Before I can stop her, she's into the lift, the doors have closed, and she's gone...

Most of us will, at some point, have temporarily lost a young child and will recognise Mary's feelings when she realised that she couldn't find her twelve-year-old son – that heart-stopping moment when it dawns on you that the child you thought was with you is in fact nowhere to be seen.

Mary and Joseph made a day's journey back to Jerusalem to search for their missing son, and eventually found him in the temple, talking with the religious leaders (a common method of religious instruction in those days). Mary's heartfelt rebuke, 'Son, why have you treated us like this?', rings absolutely true – that mixture of relief at finding the lost child and the desire to give him/her a good telling- off (although the reprimand here was tempered perhaps by the awe-inspiring surroundings of the temple and the status of the religious teachers forming the audience)! Jesus' reply is not a response born out of rebellion, but simply an explanation: 'Didn't you know I had to be in my Father's house?'

Mary and Joseph were *astonished* to find Jesus talking to the temple teachers. They had no inkling, it seems, of his inner life or the extent of his spiritual growth until now. Spiritual maturity is not related to head-knowledge or age, but to being 'tuned in' to God. Sometimes even small children will surprise us with the realisation that they have grasped a spiritual truth or even have spiritual understanding. We should not be patronising or dismissive but supportive, and, like Mary, we can 'treasure these things in our heart'.

One of my children once told me she had seen an angel 'like a rainbow'. I was about to remark, 'Oh, I don't think it could have been an angel,' when I thought, *Hang on a minute – how do you know she hasn't seen an angel?* and kept my mouth shut.

Lord, help me recognise the spiritual as well as the physical milestones in my children's lives, and to build them up spiritually as much as in all the other areas. Amen.

LUKE 2:41–52

29 LOST CHILDREN RESTORED: THE WIDOW OF NAIN

*'May the God of hope fill you with all joy and peace
as you trust in him...'* Romans 15:13

Have you ever felt that you have reached rock-bottom? The widow in this episode must have done. She had already lost her husband and now her only son had died. She must have wondered how she was going to manage, dreading the prospect of an empty, lonely old age.

As she accompanied her son's funeral procession through the town gates, head bowed, heart heavy, maybe she heard someone say, 'Don't cry.' As she looked up into the face of Jesus, did she recognise him? It didn't matter – *he* had seen *her*, recognised her plight, and felt deep compassion. She didn't even have to ask him for help (she probably thought there was no help to be had anyway) – Jesus gave her back her son.

Perhaps someone reading this has 'lost' a child to drugs, drink or some other deadly addiction. There is no situation, however desperate, which the voice and authority of the Son of God cannot reach. He sees the sadness in your heart and feels compassion for you. He is able, in his own time and in his own way, to restore your child to you. Don't give up praying. Don't abandon hope. The God of hope is also the God of the impossible, and he loves you.

Lord, you know my sadness and I don't have to explain it all to you. Please bring back my lost child. Speak into his/her situation with your voice of loving authority. Keep me hoping and trusting in you. Amen.

Pray for mothers whose children have died or are 'lost' to them.

LUKE 7:11–15

30 LETTING GO: MARY

'Do whatever he tells you.' John 2:5

When did your mum last get in touch with you to give you the benefit of her advice? Quite possibly, not very long ago! Once a mother, always a mother, it seems – at least in certain areas such as giving advice!

In this well-known story, Jesus, his mother and his disciples were all at a wedding in Cana. The unthinkable happened – they ran out of wine – and Mary turned to Jesus to tell him: 'They have no more wine.' – why did Mary make a point of telling him that? Was it just an ingrained motherly habit of passing on information? Maybe, but from Jesus' reaction I think there was more to it than that.

By this stage, Mary obviously had a clearer idea of her eldest son's power and calling. She must have known, somehow, that there was a possibility he could do something about the situation. I have heard sermons condemning Mary for her 'interference', but I think it shows a touching motherly faith in her son's ability to put things right.

However, Jesus gently responded: 'Why do you involve me? My time has not yet come.' He was pointing out to her, very graciously, that he was now old enough not to take instructions from her; he would intervene when the right moment – as he judged it – came. Mary obviously believed Jesus would act, because she instructed the servants, 'Do whatever he tells you.'

There comes a time in our children's lives when we have to acknowledge that they are grown men and women – or at least mature teenagers. We have to stop giving advice unless they ask us for it. It's very hard, especially when we see them making the same mistakes we once made! There are some things they have to learn the hard way (and some

children who never seem to learn any other way!) and some things they will only really learn from experience. In the incident at Cana, Jesus didn't need his mother's intervention, and often our children don't need ours!

Lord, help me to accept that my children are growing up and don't need me in quite the same way. Deliver me from offering unwanted advice and from lecturing them. Instead, help me to turn my natural concerns for them into prayer. Amen.

Pray for parents who find it difficult to let children go.

JOHN 2:1–11

31 PRACTICAL CARE: DORCAS

'...whoever is kind to the needy honours God.' Proverbs 14:31

Sensitive, sensible, practical –
  were you a mother whose
        grown-up children had left home?

Or someone whose motherly instincts
  were fulfilled in caring
        for other people's children?

Sometimes we appreciate the gifts
  more than the giver, until
        both have disappeared.

They crowded round Peter when you died,
  showing the small garments
        you had made so lovingly.

When you were restored to life –
  and to them – perhaps they
        appreciated you more.

**Lord, help me to appreciate people for what they
are rather than for what they do or give. Amen.**

Pray for mothers and others who feel taken for granted and
apprieciated only for what they do, not for what they are.

ACTS 9:36–41

32 | HOSPITALITY: LYDIA

'Share with God's people who are in need.
Practise hospitality.' Romans 12:13

Lydia of Thyatira,
dealer in purple cloth,
moving seamlessly between the bustling market-place
and the tranquil river place of prayer,
your heart open to receive God's word,
your home open to receive God's friends.

We don't know whether Lydia had children, but we do know that she was hospitable. We may not have children of our own, but we can use our nurturing instincts to reach out to others and offer them hospitality.

Lord, give me, like Lydia, an open heart and an open home. Amen.

ACTS 16:13–15

33 ADOPTIVE MOTHERS: THE MOTHER OF RUFUS

'Offer hospitality to one another...' 1 Peter 4:9

Have you ever been surprised at seeing a completely different aspect of someone's personality or character? Here, in the final chapter of Romans, we are suddenly made aware of a new facet to the apostle Paul. He ends his letter to the Christians in Rome by sending greetings to various relations and friends, among them a woman about whom we know almost nothing, not even her name – except that she had a son named Rufus and had been, Paul says, a mother to him as well.

In some ways it seems incongruous to think of Paul – outspoken, a great teacher and leader – needing a mother or, indeed, allowing himself to be 'mothered'! Yet here it is, from his own mouth: 'Greet Rufus ... and his mother, *who has been a mother to me, too.'*

It is fascinating to speculate how this unnamed woman 'mothered' Paul. Perhaps he stayed in her home and, with maternal intuition, she sensed that beneath the tough exterior was a man with practical and emotional human needs. She obviously ministered sensitively to those needs, treating him as a son, accepting him unconditionally, and looking after him by mothering, not smothering him. And Paul never forgot this.

As you look back on your own life so far, perhaps, like Paul, you can give thanks for someone who was a mother to you when your own mother was absent or couldn't help you. Perhaps you feel regret that you have never had children of your own. Perhaps your children have left home and you feel that you are no longer needed in the same way. I believe there is a great need for women who can be mothers to younger people away from home; perhaps God is prompting you to respond to that need. A woman's nurturing instinct is God-given, and God will channel it if you ask him to. Mothering doesn't involve nagging or giving unwanted advice! It does mean being available, offering unconditional acceptance of your adoptive son or daughter, and backing him/her in prayer. Is God calling you to do this for someone in your church or community?

Lord, as I look back on my life's journey so far, I thank you for people along the way who have been like parents to me. Show me anyone who needs the kind of nurturing I can offer, and show me how to give the kind of unconditional love and acceptance that you offer freely to me. Amen.

ROMANS 16:13

34 A GODLY GRANDMOTHER: LOIS

'Children's children are a crown to the aged...' Proverbs 17:6

I have a younger sister and two younger brothers. When we were growing up, our mother was very busy and fairly strict. She had to manage on the proverbial shoestring and, with less than seven years between me and my youngest sibling, she certainly had her hands full. She was totally unsentimental about us and could never have been described as 'doting'. So it amused us all to see what a doting grandmother she has become to her fourteen grandchildren! What happened? I imagine that, freed from having to make ends meet and sort out squabbles, my mother is now able to enjoy her grandchildren in a way that she was never able to enjoy us. She's not alone in this: many grandmothers seem to have a wonderful and special relationship with their grandchildren.

In his second letter to Timothy, Paul mentions the young man's grandmother, Lois, by name, along with his mother Eunice. They were both Jews, though we know little else about them. Paul comments on their faith and the fact that Timothy had known the Scriptures from his infancy. As his father was Greek, Timothy must have learnt his faith – in theory (the Scriptures) and in practice (living it out) – from his mother and his grandmother.

Ask anyone whose children have grown up what, if anything, they would have done differently if they had their time again. They almost always say, 'I'd have worried less about the housework and spent more time with my children.' Being a grandmother is perhaps God's second chance for us to get right with the next generation the things we didn't do too well on with the previous one!

If you are a granny, ask God to show you how best you can nurture your grandchildren as Lois nurtured Timothy. You will almost certainly have more time to pray for them than their mothers do, and you can, like Lois, introduce your

little 'Timothys' to the great stories and truths of the Bible. Maybe your grandchildren live too far away for you to see them very often. You can still pray!

The day after starting this piece, I was talking to a retired single friend who said of a young couple we know, 'What I like is that they are so good about handing the baby around for everyone to share. I'm not a grandmother, but I would like to be, and sharing their baby makes me feel like one.' So, whether or not you are a granny, someone in your community is desperate for a surrogate granny! Ask God to show you who they are.

Lord, make me the kind of grandmother you want me to be, or show me a family that needs 'grandmothering'. Amen.

Pray for societies like our own where too often older people are marginalised and excluded from family life.

2 TIMOTHY 1:5; 3:15